Dear Parent:
Your child's love of reading starts here!

Every child learns to read in a different way and at his or her own speed. Some go back and forth between reading levels and read favorite books again and again. Others read through each level in order. You can help your young reader improve and become more confident by encouraging his or her own interests and abilities. From books your child reads with you to the first books he or she reads alone, there are I Can Read Books for every stage of reading:

SHARED READING
Basic language, word repetition, and whimsical illustrations, ideal for sharing with your emergent reader

BEGINNING READING
Short sentences, familiar words, and simple concepts for children eager to read on their own

READING WITH HELP
Engaging stories, longer sentences, and language play for developing readers

READING ALONE
Complex plots, challenging vocabulary, and high-interest topics for the independent reader

ADVANCED READING
Short paragraphs, chapters, and exciting themes for the perfect bridge to chapter books

I Can Read Books have introduced children to the joy of reading since 1957. Featuring award-winning authors and illustrators and a fabulous cast of beloved characters, I Can Read Books set the standard for beginning readers.

A lifetime of discovery begins with the magical words "I Can Read!"

Visit www.icanread.com fo
on enriching your child's read

D1051300

For Eden—R.S.

I Can Read Book® is a trademark of HarperCollins Publishers.

Splat the Cat and the Hotshot
Copyright © 2015 by Rob Scotton
All rights reserved. Manufactured in the U.S.A.
No part of this book may be used or reproduced in any manner whatsoever without written permission except in the case of brief quotations
embodied in critical articles and reviews. For information address HarperCollins Children's Books, a division of HarperCollins Publishers, 195
Broadway, New York, NY 10007.
www.icanread.com

Library of Congress catalog card number: 2014942789
ISBN 978-0-06-229416-6 (trade bdg.)—ISBN 978-0-06-229415-9 (pbk.)
Typography by: Rick Farley

16 17 18 19 20   LSCC   10 9 8 7 6   ❖   First Edition

Splat the Cat
and the Hotshot

Based on the bestselling books by Rob Scotton

Cover art by Rick Farley

Text by Laura Driscoll

Interior illustrations by Robert Eberz

HARPER

An Imprint of HarperCollins*Publishers*

Splat was late for Cat Scouts!

The troop met

at four on the dot.

Splat threw on his scout scarf.

He tried to tie a knot

as he shot out of the house.

"Splat, you're here!" said Mr. Mott,
the troop leader.

"We thought you forgot."

"Meet our new scout, Scott!"

said Mr. Mott.

Scott looked like one cool cat.

"Splat, I can help you
with your knot," said Scott.
Scott tied Splat's knot perfectly.
"Thanks, Scott!" said Splat.

In fact,

Scott could tie a lot of knots.

Splat could not.

The scouts worked on fire building.

Scott's fire was good and hot.

Splat's was not.

Splat wished he had

Scott's scout skills.

"Okay, scouts!" said Mr. Mott.

"Tomorrow is our big hike!

Let's plot it out on a map."

"I've hiked this trail a lot,"

said Scott.

"This is a great spot!"

Back at home, Splat said,

"Mom, there's a new scout.

He's very cool.

His name is Scott.

He helped me with my knots.

I think he's a hotshot!"

Splat smiled.

"I cannot wait to hike with Scott!"

he said.

The next day, Splat got ready.

"What would Scott bring?" he said.

Splat did not know,

so he packed a lot!

When the scouts set off on the hike,
Splat walked right behind Scott.

Soon it was time to stop for lunch.

The scouts got wood for a campfire.

Some scouts got twigs.

Some scouts got rocks.

"I brought soup," said Mr. Mott.

"Have you got the cook pot, Scott?"

Scott looked in his pack.

"Oops," said Scott. "I forgot!"

The other scouts moaned.

"We can't eat soup without a pot

to make it hot!" said Plank.

Splat stepped forward.

"I brought a pot!" he said.

"I also brought some apricots.

We can eat them

while the soup gets hot."

"Well done, Splat!" said Mr. Mott.

On the hike back, Scott led the way
across a log bridge.
Splat trotted along behind him.

With each step,

the log shook—a lot!

And there was a slippery spot

where it was starting to rot.

Splat saw it, but Scott did not.

He was busy with some bugs—*swat!*

"Look out, Scott!" said Splat.

It was too late.

Scott fell into the mud!

Everyone tried to help Scott out.

But they could not reach far enough.

Luckily, Splat had a rope!

He tossed one end right to Scott!

"Good shot, Splat!" said Scott.

Splat tugged on the rope.

He pulled with all his might.

The rope started to move!

Scott went up

and Splat went down—

SPLAT!

Splat didn't mind the mud.

He had helped Scott!

The scouts rinsed them off.

"Thanks, Splat," said Scott.

"I wish I was as prepared as you."

"Great teamwork, scouts!" said Mr. Mott.

"And Splat, you are one prepared

Cat Scout.

All the things you brought

really hit the spot!

Why don't you lead us home?"

And Splat did!